DUE DATE

10/07

The FLOWER Alphabet Book

Jerry Pallotta

Illustrated by
Leslie Evans

Charlesbridge

This book was written especially for Nana King
mother of 5, grandmother of 29, great grandmother of 45 and . . .
—J. P.

Text copyright © 1988 by Jerry Pallotta
Illustrations copyright © 1988 Leslie Evans
Artist's notes copyright © 1988 Leslie Evans

Published by Charlesbridge
85 Main Street
Watertown, MA 02472
(617) 926-0329
www.charlesbridge.com

Library of Congress Cataloging-in-Publication Data
Pallotta, Jerry.
   The flower alphabet book / by Jerry Pallotta; illustrated
by Leslie Evans.
      p. cm.
   Summary: Describes a variety of flowers from A to Z,
beginning with the amaryllis and concluding with the
zinnia.
    ISBN-13: 978-0-88106-459-9 (reinforced for library use)
    ISBN-10: 0-88106-459-9 (reinforced for library use)
    ISBN-13: 978-0-88106-453-7 (softcover)
    ISBN-10: 0-88106-453-X (softcover)
1. Flowers—Juvenile literature. 2. English language—
Alphabet—Juvenile literature. [1. Flowers. 2. Alphabet.]
I. Evans, Leslie, ill. II. Title.
QK49.P127   1991   89-60422
[E]—dc20   CIP
                               AC

Printed in Korea
(hc) 10 9 8 7 6 5 4 3 2
(sc) 10 9 8 7 6 5 4 3

*The illustrations in this book are dedicated to the
memory of Robert R. Rathbun, an inspirational
drawing teacher and a delightful person.*

A is for Amaryllis. An Amaryllis is an excellent flower to give someone as a gift. It starts out as a bulb and grows to become a beautiful trumpet-shaped flower.

B is for Buttercup. Buttercups have petals that are yellow and shiny. People say, if you put one under your chin and it reflects yellow light onto your skin, it means you like to eat butter.

Bb

C is for Crocus.
The Crocus is often
the first
flower of
spring. It is
common for a
Crocus to get
caught in a late
snowfall or
even a blizzard.

D is for Daffodil. Some consider the Daffodil to be the flower of hope. Once Daffodils are blooming, everyone hopes that the cold weather and winter are long gone.

Dd

E is for Edelweiss. The Edelweiss is a fuzzy white mountain flower. It is a wonderful sight to come upon after a hike through rugged mountains. Someone once wrote a song about the Edelweiss.

Ee

F is for Fruit Trees. Fruit Trees are special. They blossom in the springtime, and later in the year they bear delicious fruit.

Other trees blossom, but the fruit they bear is not usually eaten by people. Let's not forget to get back to the alphabet.

F is for Forget-me-not. Do you think that Forget-me-not has a funny name? Whoever named this flower must have forgotten what to call it.

G is for Gladiolus. Gardeners find
that these flowers are easy to
grow. Bees must love
them because they
have so many
flowers close
together on
one stem.

Gg

H is for Hollyhock. Young children in the olden days liked to make dolls with Hollyhocks. The buds would be used for heads, and the petals would be turned upside down to make little dresses.

I is for Iris. Iris is the name of this flower. Iris is also a girl's name. Rose, Heather, Lily, Violet, and Daisy are flowers that are also girls' names.

Ii

J is for Jasmine.
A properly planted
Jasmine can be a
lovely hanging
plant. Jasmine is
used to flavor tea.
It is also used to
make perfume.

Jj

K is for Kangaroo Paw. These flowers resemble the hands of kangaroos. Some other flowers with silly names are Lion's Ear, Goat's Beard, Elephant Heads, and Pig-squeak.

Kk

L is for Lilac. Lilacs grow on bushes. They have a wonderful scent, but some people do not like them because Lilacs make them sneeze. Some other flowers also make people sneeze.

Ll

M is for
Marigold.
Believe it or
not, chicken
farmers feed
Marigolds to their
chickens so that the
chickens will have
healthy looking
yellow skin.

Mm

N is for Nasturtium. These flowers and their leaves can be eaten. People like to put them in salads, and some like to mix them in butter.

Nn

O is for Orchid. Orchids are flowers that can be worn on a dress or pinned on a lapel. They are perfect for weddings and other formal occasions because they last a long time after they have been cut.

P is for Pansy.
Pansies are dainty
delicate flowers.
When in
bloom, they
look like cute
little faces.
Pansies look
nice in
window
boxes.

Pp

Q is for Queen Anne's Lace. This flowering weed is shaped like fancy white lace. It is a wild carrot, but you should probably not eat it.

Qq

R is for Rose.
Roses smell great
and look great.

Watch out though!
Roses have
terrible thorns!
Be careful
when you
pick them.

Rr

S is for Sunflower. Sunflowers can grow taller than even the tallest men and women.

Their seeds can be eaten by people. Birds, squirrels, and other animals also love to eat them.

S s

T is for Tulip. Tulips come in all different colors. Sometimes looking at a field of Tulips is like looking at a rainbow.

Tt

U is for Unicorn Root. There are not many pretty flowers that begin with the letter U. The Unicorn Root probably got its name from the mythical unicorn horn.

Uu

V is for Violet. Violets do
not necessarily have to
be violet in color.
Some violets are
yellow, white,
blue, or red.

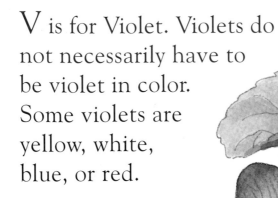

W is for Water Lily. If you were a frog, the Water Lily would be your favorite flower. Water Lilies grow in the water.

X is for Xeranthemum.
Xeranthemum is
almost as hard to say
as Chrysanthemum.
These flowers keep
most of their colors
when they are dried.

X x

Y is for Yucca. There are different kinds of Yuccas. The Yucca on this page can be found in the desert. They are visited by a special insect, the yucca moth.

Z is for Zinnia. A garden looks really pretty when it has zillions of Zinnias in it.

Uh-oh! Here come some bees looking for these flowers.

The End

Artist's Notes

A. **Amaryllis** is a shepherdess in classical Greek poetry.

B. The **Buttercup** is also known as *crowfoot*.

C. **Crocus** means *saffron* in Greek. Saffron, from the saffron crocus, is used as a spice in food and was used by the ladies in the court of Henry I of England to dye their hair.

D. A leek in the Welsh language is *cenhinen*, and **Daffodil** is *cehinen Pedr* or Peter's leek. According to legend, when St. Peter came to Wales he picked a leek from a hillside and it miraculously turned into a daffodil.

E. Traditionally, Alpine mountain climbers wear **Edelweiss** in their hats as a proof of their mountaineering accomplishments. The song *Edelweiss* was written by Richard Rogers and Oscar Hammerstein II for the play *The Sound of Music*.

F1. **Fruit trees** (apple, cherry, orange) In the late eighteenth century, John Chapman, alias Johnny Appleseed, became a legendary American folk hero through his efforts of planting apple orchards in the western territory. The lower right border shows the tidal basin and Jefferson Memorial in Washington, D.C., ringed by blooming cherry trees.

F2. **Flowering trees** (camellia, magnolia, dogwood) In the left border is Sarah Bernhardt, a French actress famous for her role as Marguerite Gauthier in *La Dame aux Camelias* in the 1880s. A film version, *Camille*, was made with Greta Garbo in the title role in 1937.

F3. The **Forget-me-not** is also known as *mouse-ear* due to the shape of the leaves on some species. One German tale explains the origin of the name. A knight, while walking with his lady by the river, leaned over to pick a flower, lost his balance, and fell into the river. Before being swept away and drowned, he managed to throw the flower to her and plead "Forget me not!"

G. The name **Gladiolus** is derived from the Latin *gladius*, meaning "sword." The gladiolus is known as the *sword lily*, referring to its sword-shaped leaves.

H. The petals of the **Hollyhock** have been used to cure coughs and to color wine.

I. The brightly colored **Iris** is named for the Greek goddess, Iris, goddess of the rainbow. The iris was considered a symbol of power by the ancient Egyptians, who displayed it on the brow of the Sphinx. The fleur-de-lis, symbol of the French monarchy, is also derived from the iris.

J. Certain **Jasmine** flowers are used in flavoring tea and scenting perfume.

K. The **Kangaroo Paw** is the state flower of Western Australia.

L. **Lilacs** were introduced to North America by the early European settlers. Both George Washington and Thomas Jefferson record in their garden diaries the transplanting of lilacs on their estates.

M. The name **Marigold** is probably in honor of the Virgin Mary—Mary's gold. Marigolds are useful in vegetable garden borders to keep insect pests away, due to the strong scent of the blossoms.

N. The **Nasturtiums** in the side borders are drawn from those in the balconies of the Isabella Stewart Gardner Museum in Boston, Massachusetts.

O. The lady's slipper is a wild **Orchid**. The vanilla bean comes from the *vanilla planifolia* family of orchid.

P. Some **Pansies** are also known as *heartsease*. It was the juice of the wild pansy (or *love-in-idleness*) squeezed into Titania's eye that acted as a love potion, causing her to fall in love with Bottom in *A Midsummer Night's Dream* by William Shakespeare. In addition, British folklore claims that picking a pansy on a beautiful day will cause rain to fall.

Q. As well as *wild carrot*, **Queen Anne's Lace** is also known as the *devil's plague*, because of its pervasive weed tendencies and again as *bird's nest*, due to the shape of the dried flower cluster.

R. On the lower right border is the Tudor **Rose**, the combination of the white rose of York and the red rose of Lancaster at the conclusion of the War of the Roses in the fifteenth century. Also, the Jacobite cause of Bonnie Prince Charlie was associated with a white rose. The roses on the top border are called *rosa rugosa* and are commonly found along beaches. The legal term *sub rosa* refers to the ancient custom of hanging a rose in the middle of a chamber's ceiling and swearing the occupants to secrecy *under the rose*.

S. The **Sunflower** is the symbol of the Sun-god in the Inca culture. In the lower left border is Machu Picchu, a spectacular Incan fortress in Peru. In her book, *My Ántonia*, Willa Cather mentions a legend that tells of the Mormon exploring party dropping sunflower seeds along their route westward to provide a floral path for others to follow.

T. The **Tulip** is the national emblem of Holland.

U. The **Unicorn Root**, originating from South Africa, grows best in frostless regions or in a greenhouse.

V. The **Violet** was the emblem of the French Bonapartists, a symbol of hope for Napoleon's return from exile at Elba. Napoleon was known as "Caporal Violet, the little flower that returns with Spring."

W. The top border shows a view of Monet's Japanese footbridge over his **Water Lily** pond at Giverny and ancient Egyptian symbols of the lotus. Although the lotus is technically not a water lily, it is in the same family. On the lower left border is the world's largest water lily, the Royal water lily or the *Victoria amazonica*.

X. **Xeranthemum**, also known as *everlasting*, derives from the Greek words *xeros* (dry) and *anthos* (flower).

Y. **Yucca** fibers were used by American Indians in making baskets, and the petals are used today in soups and salads. The desert-blooming yuccas are dependent on the yucca moth for pollination. The yucca flower is the state flower of New Mexico.

Z. **Zinnias** originally came from Mexico and were named after an eighteenth century German professor of botany, Johann Gottfried Zinn, who is pictured in the top border.